Aunts & Uncles

(and Other Refugees Under the Moon)

~Selected Poems~

Eric French

Blue Mustang Press
Boston, Massachusetts

First printing

Cover Image by Jeff Gandee

Interior Illustrations by Peter French

Back Cover Photo by Michael Tully

ISBN 978-0-9759737-9-0
PUBLISHED BY BLUE MUSTANG PRESS
www.BlueMustangPress.com
Boston, Massachusetts

Printed in the United States of America

To my wife,
The loveliest woman I've ever fooled.
And to those three little girls
I'm unable to…

Contents

Aunts & Uncles

(and Other Refugees Under the Moon)

~Selected Poems~

Eric French

At the Seaside

At the seaside
the average women remove their shoes
and are reminded of the peculiar personalities
of their feet.

They wonder
whether the flaws in their feet represent something
more intrinsic to their character
than the mere misshape of bone.

They are standing there together,
at the seaside,
waiting for the blanket to lay well before them,
waiting for the nuisance of the seagull to come, which does come,
gulling there among them against the warm wind.

The average women then look out
at the brown backs of young men running to the sea,
and they choose one or two of them
as a daydream to doze to.

By a certain age,
these women
at the seaside

finally tire of doing this,
and so begin their endings heroically.

You can hear them then-

looting the gloom of Sunday mornings
for the rest of us,
unburdened by the tyranny
of vanity and shape,

as if longing
were just some poor hairstyle
you could put a hat over
and defeat with aplomb.

Funeral

My wife's aunt just died
demurely at 75,

a mere three days
before Christmas.

She had no children,
her husband had died suddenly
way back during the Iran-Contra hearings,

so those of us in our thirties
felt that it was for the best, really,
figuring that she had little to live for fully
between quiet meals alone with the evening news and the
dishwasher.

The Funeral
began with a song
by a beautiful black woman
who knew something about heartache
and a good deal about white, youthful assumptions.

Later when Carol began the eulogy
she just lost it- sobbing and starting and failing again
which surprised most of us,

except the singer
who just nodded over and over, looking down
with the most modest
expression of understanding I've ever seen.

And I saw then,
in a visit of real emotion,
how the idea of the angels came about,
and how well cast they are
as wide-outs for our deep, left-handed bombs at the moon.

And just like that
the funeral ended

and we walked outside, and the clouds were poorly drawn
and shocks of frigid wind came at us

and we scrambled to our cars like living things,
worried only for ourselves again,
failing there under such a zip of weather
in the parking lot,

just as the elderly, under our care
feared we would.

The loneliness of laundromats

isn't so lonely
if you close your eyes
and you're putting quarters into a parking meter instead
in Paris, in June
where a young woman walks by
and says, "Hello, I've been waiting for you."
and you follow her
as she leads you through Montmartre
and takes you into a quaint tenant building and then up a narrow stairwell
that makes you ask, "Was this the servant's stairway in the 19th century?"
and she looks back at you a little out of breath
and answers, "No, we're only going to the *9th* floor, you sweet man."
and you say "Oh."
and you get to the ninth floor and it's fantastic,

she's about to open a door that you feel could open into something
beautiful…really transforming
and then she says something that sounds like, "Ready?" but you can't quite make it out,
and you ask her, "What did you say?"
and she is still there holding on to the doorknob, ready to turn it

and she lifts the back of her skirt a bit as she answers you
but you still can't make it out

and then some guy says,
"Hey, I think your clothes are ready, man."

*

the loneliness of laundromats
is easily solved
with enough quarters,

or at least with enough imagination
under just the right cycle

perhaps *Delicates* will work for you
if not
try something else, something bold
like robbing a bank
or a convenience store
the next time you're in Paris,

they don't have guns there, you know
just bouquets of loneliness
and quarters that are worth a lot more
than the ones you just lost
in the unplugged dryer

an ocean behind you.

Looking thru The Dictionary of Garden Plants

is sort of like looking through God's sketchbook,

as if you're peering over his boney shoulders
as he sits there on the velour sofa, in your study
conjuring another idea
to throw into your garden.

Sometime later, say a Tuesday in July
you'll be in the backyard
watering the new hydrangea
and the lemon zest petunias, all motivated,
only to come across a new variation growing
in between them,

and you'll be confounded over its heartiness,
its weak, pale flowers,
and the question will come–
        whether it's a weed trying to fool you
        or an actual flower you can buy somewhere.

And before you pull it

you'll deem it a weed
like the rest of us do,

because it just became one day, improbably
by its own accord,
shooting up between your hydrangea and petunias
while you were out doing other things.

And that nameless thing you'll feel
as you pull it,

will be that same nameless thing
that separates you

from the inimitable soul
who knew to put it there.

The guy who rode a bicycle around the world

There was a guy
who rode a bicycle around the world
in the 1880's.

He started in California,
and had a lot of trouble, of course
when he hit the Sierra Nevada Mountains.

There were only rugged wagon trails
to use through the Sierras
so he decided to ride along the railroad tracks
which was a wise things to do,
until the freight trains came by without warning,
straight at him.

But he survived the Sierras
and eventually made his way by steamer
all the way to Europe,
which turned out to be rather good to him.

They greeted him there as a novelty,
the Euros being much more impressed by novelty then
than they are now.

A good deal later
he found himself in Tehran

where he was seen
on his shiny bicycle
by the locals
as some kind of moustached deity,

this part of the journey was
particularly sweet for him,
considering all that failure
he'd had on earth,
way back across the Atlantic.

When he rolled into China
the Chinese saw him quite differently
than the Persians did,
and they threw stones at him, trying to kill him,
because his thick moustache
hid his mouth
and his salutatory smile
in a way they weren't used to.

As an older man
he admitted that
he was very lucky to ride out of China alive.

O~O

I've been thinking about this guy
all morning,
trying to spin his story into an allegory
about imagination

and endurance
and big picture thinking
for my daughters,
who will be riding their own bicycles
this coming spring.

Though, I'll tell you,

I keep getting stuck on
the steamer he took across all the oceans
and just how I'll explain to my girls
that the oceans don't really count,
that one can't very well
ride across the water,

but I know them
and they won't let that one go.

I'll have to lie
and tell them
that the guy who rode a bicycle around the world
rode the thing on deck
the whole while aboard ship,

even under the slip
and the pitch
and the rains
of the seven seas, no matter how bad it was,

I'll have to convince them

that the guy was riding in circles around the craft
for days and days until he made landfall.

and they'll say *Really, Dad?*
and I'll say *Absolutely*.

And they'll begin that right of passage,
believing the one about how you can do anything
if you put your mind to it

even if some of us, suffering by the window
at something like
the sameness of trees

just know better.

Reunion

all of the mosquitoes died last night.

they were curled up
in the denser grasses,
hugging their knees
and shivering
before they finally succumbed
to the first freeze
of October.

in their last moments,
before the mercury's knell,
they told each other
that they wished they had said more
about who they were
to those they loved,

and they admitted their surprise
at how brief their lives had been,
set against the measurement
of the moth's lifespan
and the other fellows they'd come across,
who lacked their brains
and clandestine approach to the world.

There was a silence
as they remembered the young
that had been lost over the weeks,
and they hoped that
that there was Something after death
gracious enough to provide reunion
with those lost to them.

The final mosquito to perish last night
worried about future generations
and whispered up at the stars,
"God help us"

*

I fought with these things every day
for poems
and peace of mind
on the back porch
this summer.

And now that they're gone
and I can write
undisturbed,
I sort of miss them somehow—

as if a spy
I was finally onto
was just killed

simply crossing the street.

A guy named James

It's interesting to hear
two unattractive women talk
about a man
at noon,

with just enough voice
to carry such sincere dialogue
to your table, over the din
of an outdoor restaurant,

interesting to hear them
continue on and on

over a guy named James,

who seems to have blown it somehow
by all accounts, letting one of them down irreparably.

I've been James
a few times throughout my life,
breaking unattractive ventricles and aortas
without intending to.

it's not something I ever took lightly
-you do lose something, breaking hearts
so similar to your own,

Ambition is the lynch pin
of such heartache,

After all,
most everyone aspires
to be with someone
more alluring than themselves,

and if that can't happen today
well, the pernicious believe it might tomorrow…

Good for you, James.

Aunt Brenda

My aunt and uncle
got divorced a while back
after 26 years of marriage to phony notions of one another.

They were ill-suited
for the routines of that queer sacrament,
and ended up
loathing what they'd created together.

They lived in Groton, Massachusetts
in a beautiful old house
that I still remember well-
white with black shutters.

The house was the kind of place
where you could write a good book,
nestled there in oaken antiquities
and sumptuous light.

My aunt had that Kennedy accent
which made everything she said back then
sound offhanded and interesting,
except, that is, to my uncle
who seemed to chew on cigarettes
just to get through those evenings.

I remember being uncomfortable in my aunt's presence,
even though I was utterly drawn to her.
I guess I felt sort of Nixonian around her;
less worldly and homelier
next to her perpetual tan and charisma.

She drank too much,
and as attractive and successful as she was back then
she seemed to be profoundly disillusioned
by something ever beyond her.

It was disturbing to see disillusionment
in such a beautiful woman,
it belied her noble features
and corrupted my early notions of the world.

*

My aunt quit her life in Groton
a month after my uncle left her.
She wrote off our side of the family,
ditched her career

and just left-
landing in coastal Maine somehow,
where I've heard she now sews quilts and pillows
with odd quotations embroidered in them, like:

Bitter is just another word for cold weather

I fear that she's sewn herself
to the peculiar sadness of Maine,
where the leaves are the first to droop
and
the first to d
r
o
p
upon the porches of September,

that's too soon, it seems
for things to fall apart
like that.

*

My uncle and his lover
just bought a home
in Palm Springs.
Cary Grant's old house is just down the road.

My aunt and uncle
live about as far apart as two Americans can
from one another.

The irony in that
is almost too easy
to possibly end with.

Eggs in the morning

It isn't so terrible
to overcook
eggs in the morning

or even that your daughter won't eat them
when they're placed there before her,

and it isn't so terrible
to pour your heart out to her
as you dress her for the day,

even if she looks at you
as if you've overcooked the morning too,
and her blueberry eyes are telling you
to just get on with it.

It really isn't so terrible
to ruin eggs in the morning

when there's so much out there
bending against your home,
trying to keep you
from cooking earnest little eggs in the morning

all for a girl

who so sweetly believes
that she understands such things,

her pig tails on guard against false entrances

just as you'd hoped.

Close call

My brother and his wife
broke ranks
with all of us this summer
and signed up for a Disney cruise,

which had us all
calling each other
and saying, "Did you hear, they're going on a
Disney cruise for Christ's sake."

but we all knew
secretly
that it was a bold move,
as if they'd just decided to cover
their hardwood floors with carpet,

just like we'd been thinking of doing.

So they are on this cruise
off the Florida coast
with their two young boys,
and a few hours in
my brother and his wife both come down
with the flu.

Luckily,
my brother's mother-in-law was onboard too,
and she looked after the kids
as my brother and his wife
took turns
shitting and puking in their cabin
on a pitching ocean liner
under the Caribbean moonlight.

Upstairs, there was a cabaret act going
and a magic show was wowing
Mid-westerners and widows
on the *It's A Small World After All* deck.

My brother was taken to the infirmary
in a wheelchair at 2:00am
in a smock
and given an IV
for dehydration,

this is my favorite Disney moment of all time.

When they returned
to Florida
and told us of their Disney voyage,
we all feigned sympathy
over the phone
at their ordeal.

We were so

pleased
to hear that it went so badly,

and we became resolute once again
about
never buying a mini-van,
no matter how practical they are,
and we pledged to never live in the suburbs
or to ever resort to taking resort vacations
to please our children,

yeah, we said,

fuck all that.

Before the ballet

Before the ballet
I was in the backyard
mowing the lawn

the sun was dropping
over the tree
that I had talked so cavalierly about cutting down
the week before, when my life was going better.

I was thinking that I couldn't cut the tree down now,
and about what the neighbors would think if I did
and all of that,
as the mower was roaring everything outside
into impossible projects and undertakings
that I really just wasn't up to taking on.

It was still so humid outside, even with the sun going down
that I couldn't stop my progress with the mower for anything,
not for bumble bees
not for crickets lazing there
not for any smaller life so engaged in the grass that evening.

I finished mowing in time to shower,
and when the water came down on me
it was then that I remembered the passing of

the bees and the crickets I'd just run over,
and I pictured their deaths in slow motion for effect,

horrible.

My in-laws arrived
as I was drying off.
I could hear them downstairs,
talking like children to my daughters.

Everyone was happy downstairs
in the living room.

Then it started to rain,
and I felt good about getting that lawn done
before the rain came.

I got dressed looking out the window
and watched the rain fall onto the roof,
and then watched it go toward the gutter
and then spill down on the backyard.

We kissed our daughters goodbye,
and I spoke to them like a child, too,
and we got in the car.

My wife talked about our daughters until we hit the beltway,
where we then said very little to one another,
lost in our thoughts about the ballet
and other things we hadn't seen before.

Before the ballet
we looked into our car's mirrors separately
to get a good glimpse of ourselves as individuals
before we became a couple again and
headed to the theatre
under the same umbrella.

I looked over at an older couple
crossing the street
ahead of us.

They seemed ahead of us.

And my wife looked into my eyes
for the first time that day
and said, "Thanks honey, this is nice."

And I'll tell you it was,
it really was.

Design and her hammer

Consider the work of screws,

how exhausted they must be,
so lightessly taut
within all the lumber
of our homes,

and imagine all the ten penny nails set against the pressure
of the things they're meant to marry,
no one aware of their devotion
but the dumb, slumbering brickwork.

and just beyond the rafters
where our dreams dither
and tumble back to us,

lie the roofing staples,
ever pinning the shingles down
against the adolescent winds
and rains of March.

it is under here we sleep

among elegant monsters
tiptoeing around our bedrooms
in houses that will outlast us

and we,
armed only
by the work done years ago,
sleep as best we can

dismissing the possible fragility
of design and her hammer
with trust in those who came before us.

though

something is there
poised in the next room,
ever and always there

waiting for us to cower

under the awful newness
of adulthood.

The Second Row of Being

There were four of us
in the car,

parked along
the railroad tracks,
under the twilight

and I was sitting
next to this girl
who talked too much
and then talked some more after that

and Jeff was there
in the front seat
next to his girl,
this brilliant blond ditz
with German eyes
and peek-a-boo breasts

and *that* was the girl
I wanted beside me that night

but all that
was impossible then,

And then the train started coming,
you could just feel it roaring near

and the girl beside me
kept on talking
as if there were no train coming

and the only thing I knew then at that moment,
the one thing I believed in sincerely at 16
was that a train was coming

so I spoke up and told her,
"There's a train coming, you know"
and she looked at me
for the first time that night
as if trains going by weren't symbolic or something...

and just like that
she shut down
and things got really quiet then in the car
as the train went through.

and then Jeff leaned over
and kissed his girl
because he could,
pinching her dumb ends
with his thumbs and forefingers
which made her giggle and buckle there
in the front seat.

and I looked left
after the caboose,
following its goneness
as it took the curve
into the trees…

And I wanted to tell the girl beside me,
so quiet and small there under the moon,
that trains going by were no big deal, after all
that they'd send another one along
for those of us stranded
in the second row of being

but I knew
it just wasn't true.

The Roaring Twenties

You just know what it must have been like then:

you, walking to the Pictures
with your girl at twilight - with a name like Doris Fontaine or Violet Mayhew,
        innocent as a ladybug,
struck by the size of the coming world as she says, wide-eyed;
        "Jeez, you just can't believe how big the buildings'r gettin' anymore, ya know?"

Lighting your smoke,
you'd calm her down with a cool-
        "Don't sweat it, Doll-baby, we're just gettin' a closer look at heaven is all"

and she'd swoon over that and want to start a life with you.

But, of course
there would be the obligatory kid on the corner
peddling the evening's papers,
yelling "Extra" as if he'd read all about it,
and somehow knew
what the real news was....

that it would all end in a whimper someday

if you believed too much
in your own progression.

!!!!

There's a reason why they added the word 'again'
to that jolly old rag, *Happy Days Are Here Again!!!*

-so we'd remember how shitty it all was yesterday
as the years roll down the 5th Avenue
                                        of the world
                                                  as a coin would do,

where every so often that kid on the corner
has a mind to pick it up, scrunch his face, and say,
"How do ya like them apples? It's only a busted old penny!"

and the look on his face will affect the woman
at the window watching him.
and her husband after that,
which will affect his secretary
the next day at work,

and soon a whole company
will be consumed with that kid's expression
without even having seen it first hand.

This is how it happens,
how popular dances named after cities and insects get ruined,

It doesn't take much,

just one expression
can change the times, Old Sport

just like that.

Systems guy

I asked my father once
when I was 9 or so,
why tire companies didn't just throw
a whole bunch of nails and screws onto the roads
around town when things got tight

-they'd be rich, I told him.

My father
explained that a certain core ethic applied to everyone,
even to tire companies,

this was the real bottom line
to consider, he said.

*

I stopped by his house today
and he was writing down ideas
on butcher paper for a colleague
to improve the mission of the United Way.

Jesus Christ, I thought, this guy is too much.

My father is a systems guy,
he believes the world is integrated
and that you and I are too,

we just don't know it yet.

If he could handcuff us together
and make us discuss why we're disconnected
he'd do it,
and do it again if need be
until we finally connected.

He's right, of course.

all of us
are linked

and lost to one another
at the same time.

Even tonight, with all my neighbors
asleep in their plumb parallelograms
from here to downtown,
I'm wondering
why they're not here with me.

I suppose my father and I
are after the same thing
at the end of the day-

I just write on smaller sheets of paper
and he wears nicer shirts than I do.

I wonder if he remembers
my idea about how to improve the tire business,

I think he does.

My mother told me he's been throwing ideas
along your sidewalks these days,

to pull you over,

to draw you in…

A seizure among us

I was about to take a final exam
in a blue auditorium,
fashioned presumably
from all of the blue things buried underground beneath us,
when a young woman
near the back
moaned and then reared in an entirely new way,
in a way that few of us assembled there had ever witnessed
before.

She fell to the floor,
possessed by some awful idea
lurking there in her bones
that was determined to spoil her rather lovely figure
and quiet comportment.

She was having a seizure,
spawned from the pressure of the exam perhaps,
or from her creator's carelessness,
or, forgivably, from trying so hard not to have a seizure
in front of so many disconnected souls.
It was heartbreaking
to see her lying there on the floor
in the throes of some inner violence
that the proctors feared

might spread to the rest of us
seated in such a strange auditorium.

You could see it in their eyes-
that helplessness that comes with responsibility
as the instructors rushed toward her, only to avoid her in the same instant.

I don't judge them for this.
I felt bad for everyone that afternoon.

Of course,
there was some guy there
who knew exactly what to do.
He performed so spectacularly
that all the women in the auditorium
fell in love with him,
and all of the men wanted to shake his hand
and slap his back,
as if he'd saved the world.
She was going to be fine, we all agreed.
It was wonderful.

When she came back to us
after a long few minutes
under that guy's care,
she looked wrecked
and exhausted.

I remember the look on her face now
as my own;
it was an expression that was so cognizant of man's limitation
that all she could do then was apologize
to those around her.
The rest of us saw her expression,
and felt that we owed her an apology
somehow,
for staring into her home like that
when we really shouldn't have.

After she was ushered out of the auditorium
to some abstract area

We gradually got hold of the personalities
we'd brought with us that day.
And before we knew it
it was as if nothing remarkable had occurred at all.

I sat there in the middle rows,
looking down through the thin cover of my exam
to see if I could make out one of the questions
if I pressed down on the paper hard enough.

And I'll tell you I actually succeeded
in making out the first question,
which really eased me
after all of that.

I thought about the young woman
and how she was doing, only after
I'd made some notes to myself
on the scratch paper
that the proctors were too rattled to watch out for.
In the back of my mind,
as the hour hand neared
the opening of our exams
I looked over at the proctors
and wondered if that woman's seizure,

you must forgive me

would potentially suspend
another exam
that I hadn't bothered to prepare for.

True loitering

There is a park on 3rd street
where the children play.

they cry and bruise
and play again,
only to cry some more
until their mothers finally
lift them
and say it's time to go home

and I watch the children
being carried to their car seats
like sacks of mortar
in their mother's arms,
soon to be mixed with juice

then it's just me,
too young for a park bench, really

loitering under the dangling evening,

wondering at
the architecture of the curved slide,
noticing the shoe marks
along its silver belly

the last thrusts
of sunlight, how thrown they seem

at the curved slide,
who's admitting to the monkey bars
that he's hoping
he doesn't hurt anyone tomorrow
like he did today

and the starlings are pecking
at the remnants of lost candy
in the gravel
as if they were looking for a wormhole south
or a better pair of wings to wear,

pecking and pecking
so shamelessly

that it seems as if
the burden of flight is upon them there,

and these birds suppose
that they could never in a million years
explain to me,

how such an ability
could ever become

such a drag.

Interior

We were painting
an interior
for a man with a troubled wife
a few months back

he had ordered all the paint himself
over the phone,
telling the rep
between apologies
that his wife was very sensitive
to the fumes of the modern paints
everyone was manufacturing these days

and the rep assured him
over the phone
that their paints were specially designed
for troubled spouses
and that she would personally guarantee
his wife's satisfaction with their product

when the paint was delivered
we found it to be shitty
and particularly non non-odorous
which had the man with the troubled wife
wiping his forehead over and over

with what to do
as we kept on working.

the special paint was expensive
he explained,
and we all felt bad for him

He was an optimist at heart
even though his wife was troubled,
and it was clear that he wanted to dump her,
we just knew it
but he couldn't, because he loved her
and we knew that too

who wants to start over
so deep into their movie anyway

He told us that he spent his afternoons
at the karate school on Jefferson Street
trying to get from brown belt to black belt

we were surprised that a man pushing sixty
would bother with such things,
and then he told us about his time in Vietnam
and how heavy it all was there
so we understood why he would waste
his time that way.

When we finished the work
on his interior

he was very pleased with our attention
to all the details,
and he was plaintive and low voiced
as we gathered our tools
and walked out of there.

As we were leaving he said he'd let us know
if his wife reacted to the paint fumes,
and we said, *Yeah, do that*

we wished him well
as we got into our trucks

Bob lit a smoke and said,
he's a goner
and Ken said,
yep, it's too bad

and I drove home thinking about
all of us for a mile or two,

as if we were somehow
all in this together.

Sinatra

is there
for you,
in stereo, in the wee
small hours
when you hit that age
your father was better suited for,
the one that really
turns you,
just enough
to remember
the girl
across from you
in grade school,
ever across from you
walking home
across from you,
her skirt tapping
at her knees,
the sun all
over her,
she's yours,
go talk to her,
well, maybe tomorrow,
tomorrow is yesterday
and for today
they made
Sinatra.

After the ballet

After the ballet,
in that jolt back to wipers and blinkers
and the beltway home,
we find our lives returned to us
like checked coats we're surprised to see again.

In the lull at the stoplight,
the silence is so present
that I tell it to put its seatbelt on.

At green
we go,
my wife disappointed in our vehicle
for being the same as it was before the ballet
and she contemplates a finer one,
sliding into grander designs and standards,
uplifted from such determined elegance on stage
that evening.

I wanted to tell her during the ballet
that I thought the whole thing was forced
and overdone,
even though the dancers were really something to consider
if you watched them while they weren't dancing,
when they just stood there, gracefully

listening to the orchestra for that moment
when they were to move again.

*

After the ballet
the lights were raised
to reveal the old velvet chairs we were seated in.

and you wouldn't have thought, looking at the chairs there,
that they could ever squeak so crudely
above such delicate music.

We were all standing
in our rows, waiting for the urgency in the elderly
to finally employ
and move them up the aisles.

I'd wanted to be alone then,
in the perspective
of my car
so I wouldn't forget to tell my wife
all of the things I was sure she hadn't noticed.

When we finally got closer to the exits
the little girls seemed struck by something
and were better behaved,
everyone looked good under the opulence
of the chandeliers.

After the ballet
we pull into the driveway,
and I turn off the engine.

It is the quietest moment of the day.

Then comes the rustle to exit the car
without annoying one another,
then the forlorn tedium of the seatbelts,
the rattle of too many keys,
the reach for the wet umbrella in the back seat.

Out of the car,
I look down our street
on the way to the front door
and everyone's aslumber under the wet rooftops,
under the rain

all of us
under the rain,
under something
that theatres were so conceived
to warn us of.

On your birthday

On your birthday
we started a ceremony of sorts
for your odd self,
gave our eyes over like a policeman forfeiting his badge.

On your birthday
we sang poorly
as the sun came yellow through the kitchen window
and you saw our faces exactly, like the dentist must see them.

and on the moment
when you mattered most,

you said something about a smoke
and something about sugar
while your sister led you by the arm, birthday-girling your ear

when all you really wanted
was to finish that book.

There's something wrong with the stars

There's something wrong with the stars tonight
and something's wrong with the guys who study them,
and there's something wrong with the astronauts adrift in
between them, too-
lost as can be
miles from earth, boyhoods
away from the wind that's
warming
the continent
at long last.

And there's trouble within the restaurants as well,
trouble inside the waitresses
and the poorly dressed managers
who just can't manage any longer.

But no worry.

In the morning
the stars will bow and go home
and wipe the silver from their faces
like actors do

and the stargazers will soon remember
all that their fathers told them about the here and now,

as they drive to work
and begin their day

and the astronauts
will soon be earthonauts again
like the rest of us,
when they climb down their beanstalks
and change their minds for the first time in years
saying, *I now know less somehow with more information*

and the sensible waitresses who feed us
will surely continue on - dreaming precocious dreams
of fortune and respectability,

just as all the failed missions
who come to see them night after night,
silently want them
to achieve.

I remember meeting a red haired girl

I remember meeting a red haired girl
in a café
by the sea
on a lovely day in September.

We were both broken people
at the time I suppose,
she in her *what do I have to lose* dress
and me in my sunburn and
favorite blue slacks

And though our conversation was hustled
by things we hadn't spoken of to anyone for so long,
we believed the other whole and invaluable, it was wonderful.
We spoke for over an hour
and left with phone numbers to show the others.

I never called her.
She might've been relieved,
I know I was.

I like to think of what she did that afternoon
after our talk by the sea,
if she called her mother

or her sister
under the possibility of evening

The red haired girl
in the café
by the sea, on a lovely day in September
now seems so many oceans ago
that I think I may have married her
and lost her all over again.

Rolling Valley Mall

There is a famous photograph
from the Vietnam War,
one of those Life Magazine shots
that seem to define the times
for everyone,

It's the one where a South Vietnamese general
is shooting a man point blank
in the side of the head, on Main Street in Saigon

presumably for treason.

It's an incredible image,
the man about to be shot is contorting his face
because he knows what's coming
and he can't believe it,

and we can't either
which I guess is why the photo defined the times.

The general outlasted the war
and emigrated to the U.S.
in the mid-Seventies, he opened up
a pizza parlor of all things
in Rolling Valley Mall,
an easy mile from our house in Northern Virginia.

Me and my brother used to go there
when we were boys
and get a pizza on Saturdays.

The pizza was always greasy and wasn't very good,
but it was cheap and the service was excellent,
even at that age we knew it was superb.

It wasn't until high school
when we heard the rumor
that the man in the photo with the gun
was the same one
who smoked cigarettes by the carton
at the cash register.

When it officially came out
in the local paper
that he was indeed the general
who killed that man

everything changed.

He was never at the register after that,
you'd see him now and then pop out
of the kitchen or the office door,
but you could tell he was uncomfortable
and probably crushed to lose
his anonymity after starting his life all over again.

The restaurant closed after a follow up piece
came out a few months later
in The Washington Post.

My brother had gone off to boarding school by then
and I was just discovering what music could do for your life
so we didn't really talk about the restaurant closing
or whatever may have happened to that family.

Actually, come to think of it,
I still don't think we have.
The general died sometime in the Nineties, in his eighties
and as he was ailing
you just wonder what he must have been thinking
about this life,
how tall history must've seemed to him,
how permanent all the shadows of decision must have appeared
then.

I liked the man,
there was a dignity about him
that I hope he carried throughout his later years
despite that moment, that one moment

when the whole world decided
to sneak up
and peek in on him.

the Coral Sea

yesterday
is listing,

stem to stern
she's taking water

her sailors,
doomed

in the Coral Sea.

the lights of Port Moresby
are showing
along her surface

the stars too,
maybe the moon.

a buoy
from the last great war
remains at anchor,
still working

made by man
for the next one coming

it flashes
on, off
yes, no

today, tomorrow

a winking thing
in the sea,

brunt of wave
and wind,

an emblem of a peculiar wisdom…

the oceans beyond, it signals

are anything

but blue.

The Current

We were at the beach
that afternoon,
it had rained in the morning
but by noon
it was glorious up above,
clear and blue
cleaner than before

but the winds remained
from the morning
and the undertow warning flags
were stuck in the sand every 200 yards
to warn us
of the deep pull just beyond the shore

I went into the water,
up to my knees
and I could feel the current
trying to pull my ankles
out from under me

an odd sensation,
like the one you get standing on the edge of a roof,
so much reality coming for you
that you have to mother yourself for an instant
to get your bearings again

and then a fish or some other creature
bumped into my calf,
and I thought about how
ocean life should know better than that, that squirrels
and deer never bump into me in the woods

and that spoiled things for me right then
because I started wondering about sharks
and soon I was out of the water
walking over to my family
who were busy with sand castles
and buried legs and laughter

*

when we got home
we heard on the news
that a woman had drowned
after we left,

she was in her mid-fifties
and married to a younger man in his early forties

she had come to Charleston
for her high school reunion
and she went out that afternoon
into the water with two old girlfriends
and her husband

The current
pulled them all out to sea together

the other two women managed to find
a way out and started to swim back to shore

the woman's husband found his way out too
and left his flailing wife
on her own
to sink or swim

she sank like a stone
from exhaustion
before the strapping lifeguards could get to her

her two friends from childhood
were reportedly devastated,

and her husband, Jesus,
who knows what he was feeling,
the news anchors didn't even touch that one.

I wonder if the husband felt that pull
when he walked into the water like I did,
whether he worried about
the current
that I can't ignore anymore these days,

he probably did, and still went out anyway

there's dignity in that, at least.

There is such a thing

My first heart,
probably like yours,
failed to keep her
and thumped off to Spanish lands
to mumble things only babies could understand
and baby was that tough, tough.

my second heart caught up to the first
around Miami, I think, and gave it a good a talking to
and ended up never coming back neither,
I heard it went for some Brazilian bossa nova singer
who turned out not to be the sensitive lush it'd hoped for,
dumb.

my third heart was a good heart,
maybe my truest heart
and left me flat
for the everything of an actress
on a Sunday too good for the gauche
too lean for the heavy
too bold for California.

this heart remembers the others
like we do past politicians,

with respect and a little attitude,
warmly contemptuous if there is such a thing,

there is such a thing.

If you look hard enough

Our friends have an old farmhouse
nestled in the dip of a valley
that spreads westward towards the Blue Ridge.

From the back porch
you can make out a few horses
if you look hard enough,

and you can see the quiet tonnage of cows
across the fields,
with their heads all pushed down to the grasses,
weighted by their girth of brains
that know nothing of the invention
of sandwiches, or the brevity of assembled meals.

Our friends showed us around
the inside of their farmhouse
and I was drawn to its usefulness immediately,

everything seemed to have its place,
all the books were bunched together
standing at attention, their spines
easy to read if you tilted your head just so.

We had dinner together, the kids were playing
in the playroom
the sun began to set beyond the window.

We went to some sort of parlor after dinner
just off the dining room, among more books
and I pulled out a few that I knew.

As we began to talk
we connected over narratives
I hadn't thought of for years,
and they liked that I admitted to them
how I hadn't thought of those stories
as I should have over the years,

and as the evening was ending
I brought up an old movie I'd just seen on cable
and I asked them if they'd caught it that night too
and they said, *Oh, there must be some mistake, we don't have a television.*

I couldn't believe they didn't have a television
so I said,
I can't believe you don't have a television

and they laughed
when they picked up on how
it had never occurred to me
that there was a choice in such a matter.

Driving home,
the night was everywhere
beyond the headlights

and I was quieter
than usual after that much wine,
and Karen was too.

It was a strange feeling
to wonder about what you really need to get through it all,
what you really need to knock down the pins
of boredom twilight after twilight-

especially

when others, so well framed
on a hillside all their own

don't seem to burden themselves
with such manufactured wonder.

Into the light

It would be something to be ushered along
the long, white tunnel

with dreamy instructions
to keep moving
and stay in line,

knowing that the great big answer
was up ahead,

that all I had to do
was just follow those souls in front of me
and head straight,

into the light.

It really would be something
to be told- *Wait here, you're next after the bald man*
as I'd draw in a deep breath
and square my shoulders
against the last unknown.

And then they would give the signal
that would lead me at last, headlong
through my last doorway

where they would shake me down
and go through my entire life,
forcing me to defend my thesis, coolly
in front of everyone assembled there
who'd ever lived and died.

And both of my grandfathers would be there of course,
dignified in the front row, having not seen me in years

shifting in their seats,
holding their breath,
straining to see themselves in me

as if all we'd ever done,
as if all our actions,

had such pedigree of bloodstream behind them.

Carol

Carol wishes she were taller
and that her voice
was a touch lower
for effect

in the heat of the arguments
that she has with her mother, at 35,
on holidays and family events
that she never really plans to attend.

Carol wonders what might have been
if her last lover
had a bit more serotonin in his brain
as counterpoint
to his gloom.

She tells me at the bar
that she should've
given him a pinch of sugar
to go with those cups of withdrawal
he poured for himself every morning
to fight the day's demands.

But those days in New York
were different

than the Nashvillian variety she now spends
rubbing elbows with reluctant celebrities
and other people I'd love to know.

She seems to be evening out
as a result of southern living,

though it appears
she prefers urban heartache
after sundown,
you know, to feel uneven again,
so that she can be balanced
once more
by the promise of a new lover

who's about to walk over at any moment.

Ten thousand raindrops on a bicycle

It's still raining,
seven days now
in a row

which is too much

too much
to put away
the bicycle I left in the backyard last week,
it's still leaning there against the holly tree this afternoon,
its backbone soaked, its form so bereft
of movement
that I almost feel sorry for it
here on the covered porch,
smoking a Camel like a king would, dazed,
with word that his navy's all sunk
and lost.

there's something in the bicycle's lean
against the holly tree
that keeps me smoking in my chair,
something in my tendons
that doesn't really care enough
to walk ten yards
and roll it into the garage.

There's a hundred such bicycles
in my backyard
leaning against me
on days like this,

each one
my latest work of art,

though no one seems to notice
how lithely I fuse negligence
with meaning—

ten thousand raindrops
on a bicycle,
meaning something

at long last.

In the cafeteria

In the cafeteria
the girls would show that bit of thigh - you remember,
running up from under the knee
like that stretch of the yellow brick road

and they'd dangle their sandals upon perfectly tanned feet
and they'd throw their heads back
laughing like women at the things
written yesterday on the bathroom walls.

in the cafeteria
the girls would fetch you
even though
they never really fetched you,

and most nights
you would save them from burning houses
and burning men,
with your stereo playing all soft in the corner
and no sisters down the hall
to explain everything to you.

in the cafeteria
you dropped your tray
and the fries went down

and then you went down,
and then the apple rolled an impossible length
of floor
and most everyone watched this rolling thing
of you
knocking against shoes and casters and laughter
until you finally palmed the apple
and got your tray together

and then you raised yourself and walked
to the empty table near the door,

sat down with yourself,
quietly praying to something beyond the fluorescence,

all at once,
so moved
by your aptitude for sorrow.

History Lesson - The white man takes Virginia

When the white man landed
in Virginia for good,
the men and women brought their wares
from the ships to the shore
in one great display of Western evolution,
dragging dozens of large wooden crates
filled with the essentials of the time-
like anvils and hammers and bibles,
boot-making gear, and the like.

By the time they finally got to shore the women were
sick of the ocean
and the men were sick of the songs
the women had sung during the voyage,
wishing they had just left them back home – the songs, that is.

But they were all of them glad
to be rid of those "fucking seagulls"
that had followed them
the whole way from England.

The Powhatan Indians
were watching all of this from an overlook above the trees
as the white man
lugged their wooden boxes

and jingling metal cookery
to a little clearing just beyond the shore.

They watched as a fat white man tripped over a bundle
of blankets he was carrying and then fell upon them,
his black buckled-boots flailing in the sand.

the fat man freed his arms and then rolled over onto his back-
    breathing hard
with his big mouth agape in the sunshine,
and then he just laid there for a moment to gather himself.

The Powhatan Indians laughed at the fat man
and one of the warriors said, "That shit is funny."
and they all agreed that the white man, ugly as he was, was very
    funny.

Later that day
the Powhatan edged closer to the white man's camp
to get a better look.

They were shocked
at the amount of clothing the women

were wearing, and they figured the women
were hiding something under their clothes.

They were indeed,

The natives never had a chance.

The fat man got up that day
and never looked back,
the pull of all the resources before him
consumed him in total thereafter.
And those women
had scores more like him,
stirring there in utero, under all that fussy woolen clothing.

That first night
the Indians heard the white women
singing songs about a savior without drums,
which disturbed them greatly;
it was as if the women were urging the trees toward deeper
        splendor
after the rainy season had already ended.

An elder whispered to the tribe,
"What terrible sounds they are making," and he adjusted his
        headdress,
"The spirits must be unhappy with us."
and he led the Indians back into the deeper woods
to regroup.

Meanwhile, Jesus
who was watching all of this,
put his hands on his head
saying to Paul,

"We have to start thinking this stuff through a little more."

Mum

When my dad was at sea
in the Seventies,

my mother used to threaten Dave and me
with a wooden spoon
when we would misbehave,
when her milky pleas for order
had spilled upon the floor
and she just couldn't deal anymore, I suppose.

the wooden spoon never hurt,

and I guess she knew it

but it worked, and would change
the situations just enough
to give her a little relief
on impossible afternoons
with the two of us.

Her husband at sea, my mother
raised us without council or complaint,
and she never let on
that she felt hoodwinked by my dad
at having to do so much
beyond the ease of loving her boys.

When I think back
I imagine she even took the trash cans
to the curb twice a week
while Dave and I were both adream in our bunk beds,

and I can just see her
dragging those broken-handled things
down the drive

without even a notion to look up
and see what all the stars were doing there,

up above, all for her.

The failures of others

I was pumping gas at the new gas station
on 4th Street last week
when I came up with this one-

The failures of others

a brazen title, I'll admit
but a subject dear to my heart
and one that I thought I would take on later,

with due care in my back yard
with my view of the old days
and the universe in full,
both on loan to me
for an hour or two
with such a subject to consider.

*

There was a guy in the next bay over
pumping gas that day
who looked kind of like me.

Impatient with the slowness of the new gas pumps,
the guy went inside the store

to get a donut that I sensed
he didn't really want.
He came back out to his car,
saw me, and nodded in the affirmative.
I met him halfway, nodding back coolly.

We both felt pretty good after that.

Emboldened from our exchange
he started his car
like cool guys do,
looking up and to the right - wincing a bit,
like it's hard to start a car.
He took a good bite of that donut,
and he put it in gear and pulled away.

His exit was performed in such a way
that should have left me
and any others watching
with a quiet remainder of regard for him,
like that regard given John Wayne leaving town on his horse-
irascibly bored and restless over the emotional things
us town folk waste so much time over.

That is what should have happened.

but that's not what happened.

There was loud "pop" as he pulled away
followed by the dull clink of heavy metal
hitting concrete.
He had wrenched the gas hose
from the filling pump and dragged it
a dozen yards before he realized
what he'd done.

I expected the whole station to blow,
probably due to all of those tv shows
I'd watched in the early 80s.
I sort of hunched over,
as if the gunfire would begin at any moment.

As it turns out,
nothing really happens if you pull the hose
from the pump itself,
they have invented some safety valve
so that nothing will spill,
and nothing did
-no fire, no screaming,
no nothing to change your life.

The guy was just devastated.
I saw his eyes as he looked back out of his car window
and they were opened completely to the world
and everything and everyone in it.

He thought of his wife, and family
and Chernobyl

and he weirdly recalled a Fatty Arbuckle
documentary he'd seen on PBS
in November,

he had understood something profound in an instant.

An Arab attendant from inside the store
who'd seen the whole thing,
ran out
and approached him.

The guy got out of his truck
and said despondently, "Sorry, I...forgot to put the pump back."
and the Arab attendant tended to him
in a beautifully untrained way
by asking him,
"Why you do that?"

And I wanted to go over there
and tell the Arab the reason,
I wanted to tell him all of the
ten-thousand reasons
that he'd done that,

but the handle clicked
on my particular pump

and I was free to go.

I got in my car
and started the engine
like an old woman might have done,
with no want of publicity
in any form from anyone.

I pulled away
and soon found the highway home.

I lit a smoke
and winked in a knowing way
at the great creator up there above the blue,

and as I went under the overpass,
I was thanking him aloud

so relieved
that it was wasn't my turn
to perform for him
that day.

When plastic mattered

Years ago,
I used to cut those clear plastic six-pack holders
into several pieces
after the snap of the sixth beer
on my way to the trash can.

They had informed us
sometime during the Reagan years
that those plastic things
were killing dolphins, or trapping them somehow,
I can't really remember exactly
but I know there was some depressing negative
that had to do with dolphins and intact six-pack holders and me.

This was around the time when PETA
was really shaking things up
and going strong.

I've never been a joiner
but I jumped in with that animal rights group
in my own vague way
after seeing a singer implore
the audience at a benefit show in D.C.
to treat animals better.

That was simple enough, I thought
so I pledged at that show
to start treating animals better.

I began
the next day by smiling at dogs
that passed me on the sidewalk
in my neighborhood.

If I saw a cat on the top of a headrest
looking out of my neighbor's front window,
I waved at it warmly.

I took our Cocker Spaniel, Molly
for more walks,
and let her sniff signposts as long as she wished to,
never pulling on her leash at all.

I should include here
that I was early into seeing a girl then
who was way better looking than I was
and who was ***very*** into PETA.

She became impressed with my activism
and started taking me more and more seriously
in the weeks that followed.

After a while, it became clear
that we were going to last,
whether dolphins were injured, or not

so I dropped the doggy smiles
and ignored the cats I saw in the neighbor's windows
-I don't like cats
and they've never really taken to me either, for that matter

no one likes anyone who doesn't like them back.

*

I stopped cutting those plastic holders
a few years ago,
when I finally stopped thinking of that girl for good.

and my wife, bless her
never gives a second thought
when I throw those things away uncut.

It's funny how things turn out.

There's so much coming at me now
that's worse than what those dolphins
were up against that year, when plastic mattered

and so little else did,

beyond a young girl under your arm
and a few dreams left in your pockets

to fool her with.

The drive home

The yellow barn on the drive home
with the tin roof and weathervane,
against the hill where the cows motion and the sun rolls down.

At seventy you'll think of this
as your wife breezes by you to get to the phone,
and you'll sit there on the porch
with the newspaper and the dog,
thinking of the red car you drove that fall,
past the yellow barn.

The drive home
below the white winter moon,
listening to the radio and looking for deer.

At eighty you'll ponder this
as your grandson asks you about your day
and you'll smile saying it was much different then,
though he meant today

And your pale frame will make him think
that you took a wrong turn somewhere,

and you did, you did.

John Ashbery

I've never cared for your poems much.

I've only read about five though,
through the years
in the New Yorker,

but I read the article on you
in the November issue
and it moved me,
so I returned to those poems
and I reread them,

and still didn't really like them.

I like your eyes though,
and how you still live in New York,

that's something-
New York on a budget
in your seventies.

no one knows what color my eyes are
or what's wrong with my poems.

so it goes.

my eyes are greener than yours
if you're wondering

and my poems,
well, I suppose they are too.

Thanks –

Special thanks to Dana and Margery French, Uncle Dick, Uncle Gary, Auntie Helen, Aunt Gwenna, and to Aunt Brenda — — for living such complicated, heroic, and often difficult lives ahead of me - I'm so glad you were born first.

Thanks to Michael Tully, Chris Park, Carol Tully, Kelly Pawlik, Colleen Tully, Charlotte Caron, Jennifer and Torrey Sylvester, Emerson Pseudo-Alumni, Alex McPheeters, David Berman, asparagus, alcohol, Santa, Frank Sinatra, the guy who wrote the lyrics to Everything Happens to Me, World War II, and bees and crickets everywhere — — for living the same kind of lives as the ones in the paragraph above you.

Sincerest thanks to Jeff Gandee – My oldest friend and rickshaw driver who pulled me to work each day – we've come a long a way from stealing Japanese pears in Santa Barbara. You wrote these poems, I think.

To my brother Dave – for inventing the sensibility way back in Hawaii one morning.

And to Laurie Elaine Casey - who saved me from my own averageness so long ago in those perfect afternoons I'll never forget to remember. I'm still waiting for my first heart to be returned to me...xo.

Thanks to Mrs. Brookins, for blushing, and for noticing something I never would have otherwise.

And to Professor Zanka –for the gracious reply way back - *nouns and verbs, nouns and verbs* – the only advice I still keep in mind today.

Lastly, eternal gratitude to Butch and BMP.

www.ingramcontent.com/pod-product-compliance
Lightning Source LLC
LaVergne TN
LVHW020647100826
845148LV00012B/2364

* 9 7 8 0 9 7 5 9 7 3 7 9 0 *